Chrám sv. Barbory v Kutné Hoře
The Church of St. Barbara in Kuttenberg
Opposite: The Teinkirche, Prague (old Hussite Church)

Czech Proverbs

Česká Přísloví

THE TEINKIRCHE, PRAGUE (OLD HUSSITE CHURCH).

Edited by Joanne Asala

For Joanna Choi, my long-time friend,
and Zuzana Vraštiaková, who taught me my first words in Slovak.

—Joanne Asala

Front cover: The Prague astonomical clock located in Prague, the capital of the Czech Republic. It was first installed in 1410 and is the world's oldest working clock of its kind.

Back cover: People march in medieval attire in a festival of "The Five Petalled Rose" in Český Krumlov, The Czech Republic.

Acknowledgments: A special thank you to the staff of The National Czech & Slovak Museum & Library, Cedar Rapids, Iowa, and to Sheryl Nejdl, John Kuba, Jitka Šonková, and Charles Opatrný for help with the manuscript.

Select List of Consulted Resources: Many of the proverbs of this collection were gathered from citizens of the Czech and Slovak Republics during the summer of 1993, other are from *Slovanic Proverbs* by A. P. Záturecky, Prague, 1896; *National Slovanic Customs* by Luka Ilic, Prague, 1846; *Book of Slovanic Proverbs* by I. J. Hanus, Prague, 1853; *Czech Wit and Wisdom* by Pat Martin, Cedar Rapids, Iowa, 1984; and *A Collection of the Proverbs of all Nations* by Walter K. Kelly, 1879. Interior illustrations from *Cesko-Moravská Kronika*, Prague, 1890; *Alterhümer und Dekwürdigkeiten Bohmens*, Prague, 1860; *Dejiny Národa Ceského*, Prague, 1894; and *Podunajská Dedina v Ceskoslovensku*, Bratislava, 1925. Floral and egg designs by Marjorie Kopecek Nejdl, Cedar Rapids, Iowa.

Graphics by: Robyn Loughran and M. A. Cook Design
Associate Editors 2013 Edition: Dwayne and Joan Liffring-Zug Bourret, Melinda Bradnan, Dorothy Crum, and Deb Schense

Penfield Books, 215 Brown Street,
Iowa City, Iowa 52245
1-800-728-9998

ISBN 978-1932043679

Library of Congress 2010941269
Printed in the U. S. A.

Table of Contents

6   Introduction

7   Friends

11 Man's Best Friend

13 Husbands and Wives

19 The Great Outdoors

21 Law and Order

26 Religion

30 The Life of a Peasant

36 The Czech Spirit

38 Bread and Butter,
    Wine and Spirits

45 Words Spoken

49 Health and Medicine

52 Money Makes the
    World Go Around

56 Sage Words

60 The Passing of Time

Introduction

Four qualities are said to be necessary for a saying to be called a proverb: brevity, sense, "salt," and popularity. The Greek philosopher Aristotle listed three of these in his discussion of proverbs, defining them as "remnants which, on account of their shortness and correctness, have been saved out of the wrecks and ruins of ancient philosophy." A modern definition is "a short, pithy saying in common use."

However you want to define it, the short wise sayings of the Czech people are unlike the proverbs of any other culture. There is a sharp, biting wit in nearly every adage, but it is a humor that does more than entertain the listener. The wit, like the barb of an arrow, makes the proverb stick in the mind.

These proverbs do not play a part in a person's formal education, but they nonetheless are still used by parents and teachers to impress upon the minds of their children the principles of morality and clean living. Their authority is acknowledged in the fact that these proverbs have been in existence for hundreds of years and probably will be around for hundreds more.

— *Joanne Asala*

The Lion of Prague.
Detail of illustration from the title page of *Cesko-Moravská Kronika*

Friends

Blessed is the man
who has friends, but woe
to him who needs them.

Each stone you throw
at your neighbor's roof
will fall upon your own house.

A common need
unites neighbors.

For our neighbor's sins
we have the eyes of a lynx;
for our own, the eyes of a mole.

He who helps quickly
helps doubly.

The Town Hall on the Ringplatz, Prague

Never judge a friend
  by the coat he wears.

A good friend is
  more valuable than gold.

He who has a good neighbor can
   sell his house for more money.

Friendship is like wine,
   the older it is the better it is.

Do not surround yourself
   by a fence,
      but rather by friends.

Nelahozeves

Correct your friend
    when you are alone,
        but praise him publicly.

The giver adds value to the gift.

Forgive others readily, but
    don't forgive yourself as easily.

South Bohemian Costumes

Man's Best Friend

Na mrtvého vlka psi neštěkají.
(Dogs do not bark at a dead wolf.)

Dogs are wiser than children,
   they do not bark
      at their master.

Every dog barks differently.

A dog barks at the moon in vain.

Where there are no dogs,
   the wolves howl.

Kostomlaty

Do not count on the dog
to guard your bacon,
or the wolf to keep watch
over your sheep.

The dog that fears
barks more than it bites.

Husbands and Wives

Všechny starosti utiší láska.
(Love drives away all fears.)

Women will keep silent only
those things they do not know.

Love is sweet captivity.

Do not select a wife at a dance,
but from a field of workers.

A house without a woman
is like a flower without dew.

**You will suffer most
from the one
you love most.**

The one who
is first silent
in an argument
is of a noble family.

Every pot will have its lid.

Do not be a lid to every pot.

Prague

Everything lasts for a time;
a wife until death,
and the Lord forever.

He who marries may be sorry;
he who doesn't marry
will be sorry.

Early morning rain and
a woman's tears
are soon over.

Before going to war,
say one prayer;
before going to sea,
say two;
before getting
married,
say three prayers.

Kamenny Dům v Kutné Hoře
The Stone House of Kuttenberg

17

Zámek Mělnický
Castle Melnik

Never marry an old lady,
    her hands are as cold as a frog;
marry a young girl,
        her hands are as warm as
        a feather bed.

The Great Outdoors

*Jenom ve vodě se člověk
      nauči plavat.*
(Only in water can you learn to swim.)

There's no key to the woods.

*Better a sparrow in the hand
      than a pigeon on the roof.*

An early bird hops far.

*The swallow carries spring
      on her wings.*

*When the bird is being caught,
      nice songs are being sung for it.*

Zříceniny Šellenberka
The Ruins of Schellenberg

When you hear the
rustling of the leaves,
there must be a wind.

Do not look for apples
under an oak tree.

Law and Order

To live in peace, remember
to carry fire in one hand and
water in the other.

Tradition and law are sisters.

The law is like a spider's web,
a beetle can break through,
but a fly is caught.

One often goes to court
in the right
and
comes away
in the wrong.

Justice is power.

Self-doubt means
    losing half your case
        before you get to court.

Honor rests on
    the tip of your tongue.

He who goes to court over a hen
    will have to make do
            with an egg.

In the streets of Prague
Illustration from *Alterhümer und Dekwürdigkeiten Bohmens*

Prašná Brána v Praze
The Clocktower of Prague

Laws without penalties
are like bells without clappers.

The language of truth is simple.

Divide and govern.

Exiles survive by hope.

The one who accepts a favor
    loses his freedom.

Better to have
    a handful of might
        than a sack full of justice.

Kill your anger
    while it is still small.

Anger is the only thing
    to put off until tomorrow.

Religion

Žijeme, abychom Boha uctívali.
(We live to praise the Lord.)

Every sin has its excuse.

The Lord provides the grain,
  but we must till the soil.

If the Lord wills it,
  even a rooster can lay an egg.

He to whom the Lord
  has shown a treasure
    must dig it out himself.

The devil will never be a saint,
  even if he is baptized in church.

From *Česko-Moravská Kronika, Volume II*

The Lord will drench you with His showers, but He will dry you with His sun.

Not all who walk around the church are saints.

The Lord will help the navigator, but only if he rows.

Zámek Roudnice nad Labem
Castle Raudnic on the Elbe

Chrám sv. Jakuba v Nepomuku
St. Jacob's Church of Nepomuk

Do not always
expect good to happen,
but do not let evil
take you by surprise.

The Life of a Peasant

Group of peasants at Pragur on St. Johns Day.

Cleanliness is a priority,
even if you don't have
money for salt.

Praise is a spur to the good,
and a thorn to the lazy.

*If you don't use your head,
you will have to use
your muscle.*

Lost time never returns.

Time and patience yield roses.

Peasants praying before a statue of John Hus,
or John of Nepomuk, as altered by the Church

Peasants in the streets of Pilsen

Everyone drives the water
to his own mill.

You must travel over a
rough road to reach the stars.

After nightfall,
every cow is black.

Do not lean against
a crumbling wall.

Wisdom is easy to carry
on your shoulders,
but it is difficult to load.

View from Charles Bridge, Prague

That which is soon ripe
   is soon rotten.

The best-fitting clothes
   wear out the fastest.

A full sack is heavy,
   an empty sack
   even heavier.

The safe path
   is the
   beaten path.

Well begun
   is half done.

Illustration from *Alterhümer und Dekwürdigkeiten Bohmens*

A fast horse soon grows tired.

The horse desires the yoke,
the ox desires the saddle.

The Czech Spirit

Without work
there are no kolaches.

In life we sometimes laugh,
in life we sometimes cry.

I believe in what I hold
in my hand.

May the Lord grant
me a sword
and no need to use it.

If you are born for the cap,
do not wish for the crown.

From *Česko-Moravská Kronika*

Bread and Butter,
Wine and Spirits

At a strange table
   eat what you are given;
   at home, eat whatever
                  you wish.

Eat slowly
   and speak slowly,
   and you will live
               a long life.

Without bread,
   meat has no flavor.

When food tastes its finest,
   stop eating.

Detail of embroidery sample from
Podunajská Dedina v Československu

He who cannot cut the bread evenly cannot get on well with others.

(Bread was such a highly prized commodity among the Czechs that a person's character was often judged on how he treated bread.)

The way one eats is the way one works.

Prague

The spoon is precious while the soup is being sipped.

Detail of embroidery sample from *Podunajská Dedina v Československu*

When I have
eaten enough I will
lend you my spoon.

Too many cooks
overspice the food.

Sing the song of the one
whose bread you eat.

Cabbage is best after it has been
twice reheated.

If you go into the forest for a day,
take bread for a week.

Don't praise the banquet
until you are going home.

Hope is a good breakfast
but a poor dinner.

Better one's own slice
than another's loaf.

It is best to leave and go home
when we are merriest.

Víno a děti mluví pravdu.

(Wine and children speak the truth.)

Drink yourself drunk,
and in one night
you will commit
all the sins there are.

When you oversalt the goose,
you will appreciate
a tankard of beer.

Words Spoken

Vola poznáš podle rohů,
čloněka podle jazyka.

*(The ox is caught by his horns,
man by his tongue.)*

Tell it to the boar, and the boar
will tell it to the sow,
and the sow will tell it
to the forest.

Let your teeth keep rein
on your tongue.

Not every opinion
is the truth.

St. Stephen's Church of Prague

W hat's in the heart
will be on the tongue.

J f a fool could keep silent,
he would not be a fool.

You cannot outbark your dog,
   outcrow a raven,
      or outquarrel your wife.

The one who talks a lot
   is either lying or boasting.

A word which flew
   out of the mouth like a bird
   can never be pulled back,
      not even by four horses.

Our parents teach us
   how to speak, the world
      teaches us how to be silent.

A good name
   is the best inheritance.

Wall design from *Podunajská Dedina v Československu*

Better a lie that heals
than the truth that hurts.

You can travel far with a lie,
but if discovered,
how will you travel back?

With silence
you may choose
whatever side you wish.

Health and Medicine

Happy thoughts
  are half your health.

He who eats apples every day
  takes the doctor's bread away.

Illness arrives by many roads,
  but always it is uninvited.

Health is the greatest treasure.

Water is cheaper
    than medicine.

It hurts more when no one
  knows about your pain.

What was not given you
    from above
    cannot be bought
        at an apothecary.

Where the sun never comes,
    the doctor comes often.

Woe to the sick
    when the physician collects
        his fees from the tomb.

Scene from *Česko-Moravská Kronika, Volume II*

Live without excess
and you will live
without physicians.

Money Makes the World Go Around

If a man covets
   another's belongings,
      he must be tired of his own.

He who buys cheap pays twice.

He who has money
   has a devil at his door;
      he who has no money
      has two devils.

He who economizes has
   as much as three others.

In poverty there is safety, and
   therefore there is happiness.

Statue of Charles IV., Prague

Nothing seems expensive on credit.

Fridland

In all places money is master.

Not even a dozen robbers
  can steal from the man
      who is naked.

Misfortune always comes in
  by the door that has been
      left open for it.

When the beggar
  gets on horseback, even
  the devil will not catch him.

Misfortune finds its way, even
  on a dark and stormy night.

Debt is worse than poverty.

Sage Words

Čas dává, čas bere.
(Time builds, time destroys.)

Begin a project well,
and do not fear the end.

He who licks the pots at home
will never be killed
on the battlefield.

The one who sits on the ground
need not fear a fall.

To believe is easier than
investigating the truth.

Střekov
Schreckenstein

Do not jump high in a room
with a low ceiling.

Wisdom does not fall
from Heaven.

John Hus speaking to a crowd, 1414

The one who gives
teaches others to be generous.

Do not blow into a bear's ear.

It's wrong to make promises
you don't intend to keep.

By teaching we learn.

A good conscience is
  your best asset.

He who runs too fast
  will pass by his opportunity.

Even little things have
  their value.

If you can't jump over,
  crawl under.

Detail of embroidery sample from *Podunajská Dedina v Československu*

The Passing of Time

Youth is not a virtue.

What the cradle has rocked
the shovel will bury.

It is time, not a comb,
that gives a man a bald head.

Lazy when young,
beggar when old.

A young liar
makes an old thief.

A cow is only once a calf,
but a man is twice a child.

From *Česko-Moravská Kronika, Volume II*

Death alone
measures equally.

The years know more
   than books.

He who dies from fears is not
   worth a place in the graveyard.

Where there is nothing,
   even death is nothing.

The more one sleeps,
   the less one lives.

The world
   remains open
      to the young.

About the Editor and Photographer

Joanne Asala is an editor and writer dedicated to the preservation of folklore and traditional customs. Of Polish and Finnish descent, she grew up in Bloomingdale, Illinois, and earned an English and Medieval literature degree from the University of Iowa. Joanne has edited several collections of proverbs for Penfield Books, including *Polish Proverbs*. She is the editor of *Fairy Tales of the Slav Peasants and Herdsmen*.

The cover photos were taken by Joan Liffring-Zug Bourret. Penfield Press aka Penfield Books was founded in 1979 by Joan, an Iowa photographer and writer, and her late husband, John Zug, an editor and writer. Joan's photography career covers over 60 years of nature and people involved in the 1960s civil rights struggles in Cedar Rapids, Iowa. Joan was elected into the Women's Hall of Fame in 1996. She has contributed over a million negatives to the Historical Society of Iowa.

Joan took the cover photographs for this book in Prague while on a trip with Pat Martin. Pat is the author of *Czech Touches: The Czech Book with Recipes, History, Folk Arts*.

Made in the USA
Monee, IL
23 February 2021